CY

Please return/renew this item by the last date shown.

To renew this item, call **0845 0020777** (automated)
or visit **www.librarieswest.org.uk**

Borrower number and PIN required.

Libraries**West**

X-MEN: THE HIDDEN YEARS

DESTROY ALL MUTANTS

CONTENTS

X-Men: The Hidden Years: Destroy All Mutants

X-Men: The Hidden Years: Destroy All Mutants. Marvel Pocketbook Vol. 2. Contains material originally published in magazine form as X-Men: The Hidden Years #8-14. First printing 2012. Published by Panini Publishing, a division of Panini UK Limited. All rights reserved. Mike Riddell, Managing Director. Alan O'Keefe, Managing Editor. Mark Irvine, Production Manager. Marco M. Lupoi, Publishing Director Europe. Ed Hammond, Reprint Editor. Charlotte Reilly, Designer. Office of publication: Brockbourne House, 77 Mount Ephraim, Tunbridge Wells, Kent TN4 8BS. Licensed by Marvel Characters B.V. www.marvel.com. All rights reserved. No similarity between any of the names, characters, persons and/or institutions in this edition with those of any living or dead person or institution is intended, and any such similarity which may exist is purely coincidental. This publication may not be sold, except by authorised dealers, and is sold subject to the condition that it shall not be sold or distributed with any part of its cover or markings removed, nor in a mutilated condition.

Printed in the UK.

ISBN: 978-1-84653-161-3

MARVEL
marvel.com
TM & © 2012 Marvel & Subs.

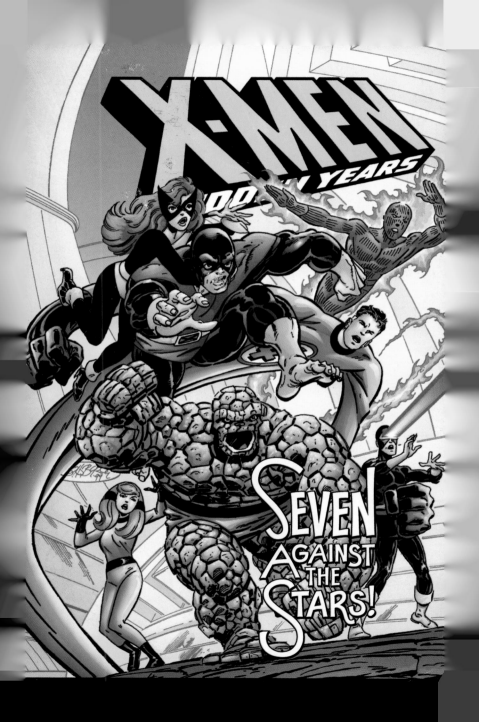

DISGUISED AS THREE WHO HAVE BEEN THEMSELVES DEADLY FOES OF THE X-MEN...

...THESE STUDENTS OF CHARLES XAVIER CARVE A DEVASTATING SWATH THROUGH THE RANKS OF SENTINELS WHO RESPOND TO THEIR VISUAL CUES...

...AND ADJUST THEMSELVES TO COUNTER THE WRONG MUTANTS.

BUT FOR THE SAKE OF THE TALE WE TELL TODAY, IT MATTERS NOT WHY THE X-MEN BATTLE THE RELENTLESS ROBOTIC HORDES...

...OR WHAT PROGRAMMING DRIVES THE SENTINELS' UNFORGIVING LOGIC.

IT MATTERS ONLY THAT THE X-MEN WILL PREVAIL THIS DAY...

...AND ESCAPE THIS MOUNTAIN LAIR, LEAVING WHAT THEY BELIEVE TO BE ONLY THE RUINS OF A MADMAN'S DREAMS!

"MY MUTANT TELEPATHY ALLOWED ME TO CONFIRM THE SINCERITY OF THE CHANGELING'S REASON FOR COMING TO OUR HEADQUARTERS..."

"...AND SO I MADE MARVEL GIRL PRIVY TO MY NEW PLAN..."

THE CHANGELING WILL USE HIS MORPHING ABILITY TO ASSUME MY FORM, JEAN.

I WILL THEN SHARE MY POWER WITH THE TWO OF YOU...

...AND THE CHANGELING WILL TAKE YOUR PLACE AS OUR LEADER!

"BUT THEN SOMETHING HAPPENED WHICH I HAD NOT ANTICIPATED."

"IN BATTLE WITH THE SUBHUMAN GROTESK, THE CHANGELING WAS KILLED...

...STILL WEARING MY FORM!"*

*ORIGINALLY SEEN IN UNCANNY X-MEN #42 - J

"THUS DID THE CHANGELING HOPE TO FIND HIS OWN KIND OF REDEMPTION!"

A MOST UNFORTUNATE SITUATION, MARVEL GIRL.

BUT THERE IS STILL A QUESTION UNANSWERED CHARLES.

...AND HE WAS STILL LOCKED AWAY, OUT OF CONTACT WITH EVEN MY NEWFOUND TELEPATHIC POWERS!

YES... THE PRECISE NATURE OF THE DEFENSE I CONCEIVED AGAINST THE Z'NOX.

I KNEW THAT IT WASN'T REALLY CHARLES XAVIER WHO HAD DIED...

...BUT I COULDN'T TELL THE OTHERS WITHOUT PERMISSION FROM PROFESSOR X...

"AS THE Z'NOX WORLD APPROACHED, I WAS ABLE TO LEARN MORE AND MORE ABOUT THEIR ALIEN NATURE.

"AND I DISCOVERED THEY WERE A RACE UPON WHOM UNCARING EVOLUTION HAD PLAYED A CRUEL TRICK.

"THEY WERE UTTERLY AND COMPLETELY WITHOUT COMPASSION.

"THEY UNDERSTOOD NOTHING BUT CRUELTY AND WAR.

"AND SO I SET ABOUT TRAINING MY X-MEN TO FOCUS THEIR INDIVIDUAL TALENTS IN A MOST UNIQUE WAY!

"YOU WILL REMAIN ON STATION UNTIL PROFESSOR X ARRIVES..."

NOT QUITE MEANWHILE, IN ANTARCTICA...

WELL, THIS TRIP HAS BEEN A BIG BUST!

WE CAME LOOKING FOR THE REST OF THE X-MEN...

...WHO CAME TO FIND OUT IF MAGNETO WAS REALLY DEAD...

...AND ALL WE'VE LEARNED FROM THE NATIVES IS THAT MAGNETO'S GHOST HAS BEEN MAKING TROUBLE DOWN HERE!

IS THAT NOT ENOUGH TO TELL YOU WHAT YOU NEED TO KNOW, HAVOK?

I DUNNO, KA-ZAR.

WHAT THAT NATIVE WOMAN SAID ABOUT THERE BEING "MAGIC" IN THE ROCKS THAT MADE PEOPLE LIVE FOREVER BACK THERE...

IF MAGNETO HAD HOOKED INTO SOMETHING LIKE THAT...

LOOK! THE MINI-CEREBRO UNIT MOUNTED IN THE...DASHBOARD IS REGISTERING A MUTANT PRESENCE.

AND NOT JUST ANY MUTANT, BABE!

CEREBRO IS REACTING BECAUSE IT'S A FAMILIAR ENERGY SIGNATURE.

IT'S ICEMAN!

BUT HE QUIT THE X-MEN...!*

*IN ISSUE 1 - J

WHAT'S HE DOING IN THE SAVAGE LAND..??

WHISPER HILL.

A PLACE OF SECRETS, MYSTERIES...

...AND TONIGHT...

MISS HARKNESS?

IS... EVERYTHING ALL RIGHT ?

...A PLACE OF DARK FOREBODINGS.

MY HUSBAND INSISTED I COME HERE WITH OUR SON, TO BE SAFE, BUT NOW I SEEM TO SENSE...

WHAT I SENSE, MY DEAR. A DISTURBANCE. SOMETHING... AT THE VERY CENTER OF WHICH ARE THOSE MOST DEAR TO YOU...!

REED! JOHNNY AND BEN!

I KNEW I SHOULDN'T HAVE LET THEM GO OFF WITH-OUT ME!

THEY HAD A MISSION, CHILD.

ONE WHICH THEY KNEW MIGHT BE FRAUGHT WITH UNSPEAKABLE DANGERS.

NO MORE THAN ANY WE HAVE FACED BEFORE...

...FACED TOGETHER, SINCE WE BECAME THE FANTASTIC FOUR!

YOU ARE FRUSTRATED THAT YOUR PLACE WITH YOUR TEAM MATES HAS BEEN TAKEN BY ANOTHER.

YES. CRYSTAL IS SKILLED, COMPETENT...

BUT WHAT I FEEL... WHAT YOU AND I BOTH FEEL...

...TOLD THE SCATHILL TEAMMATES OF A TERRIBLE THREAT TO THEIR WORLD.

THE Z'NOX USE A POWERFUL GRAVITY TRANSFORMER DRIVE TO TRANSPORT THEIR WHOLE PLANET ACROSS THE GALAXY.

LIKE SWARMING LOCUSTS THEY PILLAGE A PLANET...

...AND THEN MOVE ON!

MAKING HIS ERSTWHILE STUDENTS AT LAST AWARE OF A PLAN WHICH HE HAD BEEN FORMULATING FOR MANY MONTHS...

...XAVIER SET ABOUT HONING EACH OF THEIR SPECIAL MUTANT POWERS TOWARD A SELECTED TASK...

A TASK WHICH LINKED NOT ONLY THEIR FOUR YOUNG MINDS...

...BUT THE MINDS OF EVERY MAN, WOMAN, AND CHILD ON THE IMPERILED PLANET!

THE JOB IS DONE! THE INVADERS ARE BEATEN BACK!

I RELEASE YOU ALL-- GOOD LUCK, AND GOD SPEED!

BUT, JUST A FEW HOURS AGO...

THE AUTO-MATED SCAN-NERS IN OUR BAXTER BUILDING HEADQUARTERS RECORDED THE APPROACH AND RETREAT OF THE Z'NOX WORLD.

BUT WHAT EXACTLY DID YOU DO TO MAKE THEM CUT AND RUN, CHARLES?

HAVING LEARNED THAT EVOLUTION HAD LEFT THE Z'NOX UTTERLY DEVOID OF COMPASSION...

...I JOINED THE MINDS OF ALL THE PEOPLE OF EARTH TO TEACH THE Z'NOX WHAT IT MEANS TO BE HUMAN.

IT WAS TOO MUCH FOR THEIR ALIEN MENTALITY TO BEAR...

...AND SO THEY FLED, HURLING THEIR WORLD ONCE MORE INTO THE INFINITY OF GALACTIC SPACE.

BUT THIS WORKED NO PERMANENT CHANGE IN THE Z'NOX?

USING THEIR GRAVITY DRIVE, THEY MIGHT WELL ATTACK ANOTHER WORLD!

AND SO, TEAMED WITH THE FABULOUS FANTASTIC FOUR...

...THE X-MEN JOURNEYED DEEP INTO THE STAR CLUSTERS OF THE GALACTIC LENS...

...CHASING THE FLEEING Z'NOX WORLD BEFORE IT COULD LAY WASTE TO ANOTHER INHABITED PLANET.

UH OH. I DON'T LIKE THAT *TONE*, STRETCH. THAT'S YOUR "THINGS AIN'T GOIN' RIGHT" VOICE!

THE Z'NOX DRIVE MECHANISMS REACH DOWN DEEPER INTO THIS SHAFT THAN I ANTICIPATED, BEN.

I'M NOT SURE MCCOY AND I WILL BE ABLE TO WITHSTAND THE PRESSURE IF WE CONTINUE!

YET... CONTINUE WE MUST!

OKAY, SMART GUY, I CAN TAKE A HINT.

THIS IS WHERE MY *DEAR OLD AUNT PETUNIA'S* MOST HANDSOME NEPHEW GETS TA EARN HIS *SALT*.

JUST GIMME THE STUFF AN' A *HEADSET*, AN' YOU CAN *TALK* ME THROUGH THE LAST STEPS!

BEN...

I FEAR WE HAVE NO *CHOICE*, REED.

"*THE THING* IS THE ONLY ONE AMONG US WHO CAN HOPE TO SURVIVE THE CRUSHING *PRESSURES* SO FAR DOWN!"

BEN! REPORT YOUR POSITION. HOW IS IT GOING DOWN THERE?

WELL, IT WUZ A WHOLE LOT *EASIER* WHEN YOU WUZ PLAYIN' *ELEVATOR*, PAL.

BUT I CAN SEE TH' *MECHANISM* YOU DESCRIBED JUST A COUPLA YARDS FURTHER DOWN.

EVERYTHING PLUGS IN JUST LIKE YOU *SAID* IT WOULD.

JUST LEMME GET THIS LAST TAB A INTO SLOT B HERE, AND...

PROLOGUE:

ILLINOIS, SOME FIFTEEN MILES WEST OF THE TOWN OF DUNFEE...

NOW, KEN, YOU JUST BEHAVE YOURSELF!

FAR FROM MATTERS WHICH WOULD SEEM OF ANY CONCERN TO THE UNCANNY X-MEN...

IF YOU KEEP FLIRTING WITH BARBIE LIKE THAT, YOU'LL GET A BAD REPUTATION!

CERTAINLY, YOUNG ASHLEY MARTIN, AGE 10...

...HAS NO REASON TO BELIEVE SHE WOULD BE OF INTEREST TO THE X-MEN...

NOW ALL OF YOU FORM A RING, AND WE'RE GOING TO DO SOME DANCING.

AND I DON'T WANT ANY COMPLAINTS FROM ANYONE, THIS TIME!

IF, INDEED, SHE HAS EVEN HEARD OF OUR TROUBLED TEAM...

YOU KNOW WHAT HAPPENS WHEN I GET MAD AT...

HUH..??

WUMP

AND AS THESE FATEFUL WORDS ARE SPOKEN...

...SOME EIGHT HUNDRED MILES TO THE WEST...

ASHLEY?

COME ON, HONEY, YOU'RE GOING TO MISS YOUR BUS...

...AND I DON'T HAVE TIME TO TAKE YOU TO SCHOOL THIS...

ASHLEY?

SHE'S UP AND OUT ALREADY?

WHERE THE HECK COULD SHE BE?

ASHLEY!

OH, HI MOM.

WHERE WERE YOU? I'VE NEVER KNOWN YOU TO GET UP THIS EARLY!

I... JUST HAD SOMETHING I NEEDED TO DO.

BUT I CAN'T TALK RIGHT NOW, 'KAY?

I GOTTA CATCH MY BUS!

ER... YES, RIGHT.

SHE WAS OUT IN THE OLD BARN. THE DOOR IS STILL OPEN.

WHAT THE HECK WAS SHE DOING OUT THERE?

A FEW MINUTES LATER...

...THE HIGH SECURITY CHAMBER WHICH HOUSES THE X-MEN'S MUTANT-SEEKING COMPUTER, CEREBRO.

YES--A MOST PALPABLE HIT, INDEED, AND A POWERFUL SIGNAL.

THIS MUTANT COULD HAVE GREAT POTENTIAL.

BUT IT DOES NOT EXPLAIN THE BEAST'S CONCERN.

LOOK AT THE LOCATION TRIANGULATOR, PROFESSOR.

THAT MUTANT SIGNAL IS JUST A FEW MILES FROM DUNFEE, ILLINOIS...

"...WHERE MY PARENTS HAPPEN STILL TO RESIDE!"

I WANT TO THANK YOU AGAIN FOR THIS, PROFESSOR.

NO THANKS ARE NECESSARY, MCCOY.

YOU ARE NATURALLY CONCERNED AS TO THE WELL-BEING OF YOUR PARENTS.

I CONFESS, FOCUS ON OUR CONTACT MISSION WITH THIS NEW MUTANT...

...WOULD HAVE BEEN DIFFICULT FOR ME TO MAINTAIN WITHOUT FIRST MAKING SURE THEY WERE WELL.

WHAT ABOUT THE READINGS ON THAT PORTABLE CEREBRO UNIT, PROFESSOR?

HAVE YOU MORE PRECISELY LOCATED OUR MUTANT?

NOT YET.

WELL...THERE IT IS! CASA MCCOY!

FUNNY--IT'S NOT ALL THAT LONG SINCE I LEFT THESE PARTS TO JOIN YOU AND THE OTHERS...

...YET SO MUCH HAS HAPPENED IN THAT SHORT SPAN, IT SEEMS A LIFETIME SINCE I LAST BEHELD THIS SCENE!

HANK?

MOST PECULIAR. AT THIS RANGE THE LOCATION SHOULD HAVE BEEN CONFIRMED BY NOW.

IT IS ALMOST AS IF THERE IS SOME KIND OF CONFLICTING SIGNAL OVERLAYING CEREBRO'S SCAN.

HANK! IT IS YOU!

AND WITH PROFESSOR XAVIER, TOO! THIS IS AN HONOR, SIR!

THE PLEASURE IS ENTIRELY MINE, MRS. MCCOY.

YOUR SON AND I HAD BUSINESS IN THE NEIGHBORHOOD, AND COULD NOT RESIST A SURPRISE VISIT!

"WITH THE HYPNOTIC POWERS OF MY ALTERED STATE, I WAS VERY NEARLY ABLE TO TURN THE X-MEN EACH AGAINST THE OTHER...

"...AND EVEN SNARE THE HIGH-FLYING ANGEL TO MAKE MY ESCAPE WHEN MY ENERGY DWINDLED, AND I RETURNED TO HUMAN FORM.*

"IT WAS ONLY WHEN I CAME WITHIN A HAIR'S BREADTH OF HARMING, PERHAPS EVEN KILLING, THE WOMAN I LOVE...

"...THAT I REALIZED HOW FULLY THE EVIL NATURE OF SAURON HAD TAKEN COMMAND OF ME.

"AND SO I FLED, FLYING AS FAR AS THE ENERGIES I HAD LAST ABSORBED WOULD TAKE ME.

"AND WHERE THEY TOOK ME WAS TO THE VERY PLACE WHERE ALL MY TROUBLES HAD BEGUN.

"A FORSAKEN CABIN ON AN ICY CLIFF IN TIERRA DEL FUEGO.

"THE VERY PLACE I HAD BEEN BORN.

*SEEN LO THESE MANY YEARS AGO IN UNCANNY X-MEN #61.! – J

OH, THANK HEAVEN WE'VE FOUND YOU!

KARL!

NO! DON'T COME ANY CLOSER!

"THERE I HOPED THE RAVAGES OF HUNGER AND THE UNFORGIVING CLIMATE WOULD END FOR ALL TIME THE CURSE OF SAURON...

"...BUT I COUNTED WITHOUT THE TENACITY OF THE X-MEN...

"...AND MY BELOVED TANYA!"

STAY BACK! STAY BACK!!

"KNOWING MY HUNGER WOULD CAUSE ME TO *DRAIN* THE PRECIOUS LIFE-ENERGY FROM *TANYA* IN BUT A MOMENT...

"AND SO I *FELL*--BUT NOT AS *FAR* AS I HAD THOUGHT I MIGHT.

"AN *UNEXPECTED* LEDGE SAVED ME...

"WAITING LONG ENOUGH FOR THEM TO HAVE *MOVED* BEYOND CHANCE OF *SPOTTING* ME...

"...I INCHED MY WAY DOWN THE *TREACHEROUS* CLIFF, AND FOUND MYSELF IN A PLACE I HAD HEARD WHISPERED ABOUT IN *LEGEND*...

"...I *FLED*, SEEKING THE EMBRACE OF *OBLIVION* OVER THE TOUCH OF MY CHERISHED *TANYA*.

"...AND *HID* ME AS THE *X-MEN* DESCENDED IN THEIR OWN WAY INTO THE *ABYSS*.

"THE *SAVAGE LAND!*

"IN THE *PREHISTORIC MONSTERS* THAT POPULATE THIS PLACE I SAW A WAY TO FIND ALL THE LIFE-ENERGY I WOULD *EVER* NEED...

"...BUT KNOWING THERE ARE ALSO *PRIMITIVE HUMANS* IN THE *SAVAGE LAND*, I CHOSE TO *ISOLATE* MYSELF AS BEST I COULD...

"...AND BUILT A *CRUDE RAFT* IN ORDER THAT I MIGHT *ROW OUT* TO THIS SECLUDED *ISLE*.

LITTLE DID I GUESS WHAT I WOULD FIND HERE.

THE LONG DEAD *REMAINS* OF A *GERMAN EXPEDITION*, SENT APPARENTLY ON A MISSION TO *EXPLOIT* THE *GEOTHERMAL ENERGIES* IN THE VOLCANIC STRATA BENEATH THIS ISLAND.

YET EVEN IN THEIR *FAILURE*, THEY LAID A *GROUNDWORK* WHICH MAY PROVE OF USE TO ME...

...IF I AM *RIGHT*, AND THEIR *MECHANISMS* CAN BE *ADAPTED* TO PROVIDE ENERGIES ON WHICH I CAN *FEED*...

AND HOW WILL ALL THIS AFFECT *ICEMAN* AND HIS *TEAMMATES*, YOU ASK?

THAT ANSWER WILL COME IN DUE TIME, READER.

FOR NOW, THOUGH, WE LOOK BACK TO AMERICA, TO ILLINOIS...

AND TO...

THIS HOUSE.

A DOMICILE OF ALMOST EXAGGERATED NORMALCY, PROFESSOR! I HAVE GROWN ACCUSTOMED TO FINDING OUR MUTANTS IN MORE EXOTIC LOCALES!

YET MOST COME FROM HOMES AND BACKGROUNDS EVERY BIT AS NORMAL AS THIS, McCOY...

...AS YOU DID!

IN MANY WAYS IT IS THAT AS MUCH AS ANYTHING WHICH SPURS THE UNNATURAL FEAR SO MANY HOMO SAPIENS HARBOR FOR MUTANTKIND.

WELCOME

YES--FEAR OF THE DIFFERENT. HOW WRENCHING TO A PAIR OF NORMAL HUMANS...

...TO FIND THEMSELVES TO WHAT THEY MIGHT DEEM A MONSTER!

I SENSE NO SUCH FEARS HERE.

IF I AM CORRECT, AND THIS IS INDEED THE HOME OF THE NEW MUTANT...

...HE OR SHE MAY NOT YET HAVE MANIFESTED ANY EXTRAORDINARY ABILITIES FOR ANYONE ELSE TO SEE.

NO RESPONSE TO THE DOORBELL.

WOULD IT BEHOOVE US TO SCOUT THE TERRAIN, PROFESSOR?

YES--LOOK AROUND, McCOY.

"BUT MAKE DISCRETION YOUR BYWORD!"

PROFESSOR X CONTINUES TO TREAT US IN MANY RESPECTS AS THOUGH WE WERE ALL NEOPHYTES.

AS IF I WOULD EVER DO OTHER-WISE!

I FEAR THE BRIEF COMA INTO WHICH HE FELL AFTER OUR BATTLE WITH THE Z'NOX...*

...MAY HAVE DONE DAMAGE WE HAVE YET TO FULLY ASCERTAIN.

*SEEN IN UNCANNY X-MEN #65 - J

YES, CANDY, IT IS.

WE X-MEN DON'T WEAR OUR COSTUMES JUST TO MAKE A *FASHION* STATEMENT.

THEY ARE TO *PROTECT* OUR *REAL* IDENTITIES...

...AND IF I'M *GOING* WITH YOU, YOU *CAN'T* AFFORD TO HAVE ANYONE MAYBE *RECOGNIZE* ME...

...AND MAKE A *CONNECTION.*

FAIR ENOUGH. BUT DON'T YOU HAVE ANYTHING A LITTLE MORE *STYLISH?*

AND, REALLY, *GREEN* HAS NEVER BEEN MY COLOR!

CAN I *OPEN* MY EYES NOW, LADIES?

IT'S A LITTLE *TRICKY* FLYING THE *PLANE* THIS WAY!

ANY TIME YOU LIKE, SCOTT.

WHERE ARE WE ANYWAY?

ABOUT *FOUR* MINUTES FROM *WARREN* AT THIS SPEED.

BUT... I HAVE A *QUESTION,* JEAN.

IF YOU HAVE A *SPARE* OF YOUR *CURRENT* COSTUME FOR CANDY TO WEAR...

...WHY ARE *YOU* STILL WEARING YOUR OLD *SCHOOL* UNIFORM?

I'M NOT REALLY SURE, SCOTT. IT JUST FEELS... *COMFORTABLE,* SOMEHOW.

THERE'S BEEN SO *MUCH* GOING ON LATELY. SO MUCH *TURMOIL* IN OUR LIVES.

MAYBE THIS GIVES ME A SENSE OF *CONTINUITY!*

BUT...

TODAY...

THE PLEASANT SUBURBAN COUNTRYSIDE NOT FAR FROM THE CITY LIMITS OF DUNFEE, ILLINOIS.

NOT AT ALL A PLACE ONE MIGHT THINK TO HARBOR A SCENE OF CHAOS...

...AND IMPENDING DEATH.

THAT SENTINEL CRASHED THROUGH THIS RESIDENCE AND FELLED THE BEAST IN ONLY A MATTER OF SECONDS!

NOW IT HAS SEIZED THE LITTLE MARTIN GIRL, ASHLEY.

AND AS THESE OBSERVATIONS RACE THROUGH THE MIND OF THE MAN CALLED PROFESSOR X...

NOW YOU STOP THIS AT ONCE!

IT RECOGNIZES HER AS THE MUTANT WHOSE APPEARANCE BROUGHT US HERE!*

*TOLD IN GREATER DETAIL LAST ISSUE - J

I DIDN'T HELP YOU AND HIDE YOU IN THE OLD BARN SO YOU COULD WRECK MY MOM'S HOUSE!

YOU JUST PUT ME DOWN RIGHT NOW!

COMPLIANCE.

THIRD MUTANT READING IDENTIFIED AS MARTIN, ASHLEY.

NATURE OF POWER; UNDETERMINED.

??

THE SENTINEL... OBEYED HER! I THOUGHT NOTHING OF IT WHEN IT SEEMED TO DO AS SHE SAID...

...AND PUT MCCOY AND ME BACK DOWN ON THE GROUND AFTER CAPTUR-ING US...

BUT NOW... IT SEEMS ALMOST AS THOUGH SHE IS SOMEHOW... CONTROLLING THE THING!

ARE YOU OKAY, MR. XAVIER?

I'M SORRY --I JUST DON'T KNOW WHAT'S GOTTEN INTO MY ROBOT.

WE CAN'T GET TO THEM AS LONG AS THE *MALE* KEEPS BLASTING!

WHERE'S *KRUEGER?* HE SHOULD BE ABLE TO HANDLE THIS!

I'M HERE, MY CHILDREN.

NEVER FEAR. I AM *ALWAYS* NEAR AT HAND!

SCOTT...!

MY OPTIC BLAST JUST *WASHES* OVER HIM LIKE RAINWATER!

WHO THE *DEVIL..??*

THE DEVIL INDEED, SOME HAVE SAID, CYCLOPS.

MY NAME IS *KRUEGER.* FOR NOW THAT IS AS MUCH AS YOU NEED TO KNOW.

YOU CALLED ME *"CYCLOPS".*

YOU KNOW WHO WE ARE?

OF COURSE. I HAVE FOLLOWED THE CAREERS OF YOU *X-MEN* SINCE YOUR PUBLIC DEBUT AT *CAPE CITADEL...* ※

LIKE YOUR OWN *PROFESSOR X* I HAVE GATHERED ABOUT ME A BAND OF NATURE'S MISTAKES...

THOUGH WE DO NOT *HIDE* OUR AFFLICTIONS BEHIND POLITE TERMS OF *SCIENCE* AS YOU DO.

WE HAVE NO NEED FOR WORDS LIKE *"MUTANT."* WE ARE QUITE CONTENT TO CALL OURSELVES *FREAKS.*

※*WAY WAY BACK IN UNCANNY #1 – J*

THE SENTINEL HAS *CEASED* ITS COUNTERATTACK!

PROFESSOR..?

IT WOULD APPEAR THIS POTENTIALLY *DANGEROUS* SITUATION IS... TEMPORARILY IN HAND!

THAT'S PRETTY GOOD *JUMPING*, MISTER! HOW DO YOU *DO* THAT?

ER... YEARS OF PRACTICE.

BUT...PRO-FESSOR... WHAT IN THE NAME OF *ASIMOV'S THREE LAWS OF ROBOTICS* IS GOING ON HERE..??

I WAS ABOUT TO ASK THE SAME QUESTION!

MOM!

ASHLEY!

OH, BABY, YOU'RE OKAY! WHEN I DROVE UP AND SAW THE *HOUSE*..!!

GENETIC SCANS IDENTIFY NEWCOMER AS FEMALE PARENT OF MARTIN, ASHLEY. CODE APPELLATION *"MOM."*

NO VARIANT FROM CORRECT GENETIC MATRIX DETECTED.

BUT... WHO ARE THESE MEN? AND... AND WHAT IN THE WORLD IS... IS *THAT?*

DON'T BE *AFRAID*, MOM, HE GOT A LITTLE *CARRIED AWAY*, BUT THIS IS MY *FRIEND*.

I CALL HIM *BIG BOT*.

"*CARRIED AWAY*..."

MY... HOUSE...

ALLOW ME TO *EXPLAIN*, MRS. MARTIN.

"OF COURSE, YOU HAVE *MANY* QUESTIONS..."

MEANWHILE...

YOU... YOU THINK ASHLEY IS A... A MUTANT..??

INDEED. I AM *SORRY*, MRS. MARTIN--IT IS NOT OUR NORMAL *POLICY* TO MAKE EVEN THE *PARENTS* AWARE OF THEIR CHILD'S GIFTS.

NOT UNTIL A PROPER PERIOD OF *PREPARATION* HAS ELAPSED AT LEAST...

BUT THE PRESENCE OF THIS ROBOTIC *RAVAGER* HAS RATHER *DIMINISHED* OUR OPTIONS IN THAT RESPECT!

I'VE... HEARD OF THESE *SENTINELS*. THEY WERE ALL OVER THE TV A FEW WEEKS AGO.

SOME GUY NAMED *TRASK* OR SOMETHING...

BUT... *HOW* DID THIS THING FIND *ASHLEY*..?

THAT WE DO NOT KNOW... UNLESS...

ASHLEY... I WONDER... DO YOU THINK YOUR... *FRIEND* WOULD *TELL US* IF YOU ASKED HIM?

SURE. IT'S NOT LIKE HE'D HAVE A *CHOICE*.

BIG BOT! TELL US WHY YOU *CAME* HERE!

COMPLIANCE.

"THIS UNIT ASSEMBLED ITSELF FROM FRAGMENTS OF *FIVE SENTINELS* DESTROYED IN BATTLE WITH THE X-MEN.

"REPAIR SEQUENCES TOOK SEVERAL DAYS...

"...BUT INTACT MEMORY BANKS INDICATED REMOVAL FROM COMPROMISED BASE TO BE A PRIORITY.

"RANDOM SELECTION SET THIS UNIT ON A *WESTWARD* FLIGHT PATH.

"AUTOMATIC SCANNERS DETECTED *MUTANT PRESENCE* WHEN PASSING DUNFEE, ILLINOIS.

And DEATH Alone Shall Know My Name

MANY HAVE BEEN THE FACES AND FORMS OF EVIL THROUGHOUT THE LONG HISTORY OF THE PLANET WE CALL EARTH.

IN THE LATTER HALF OF THE 20TH CENTURY, HUMANITY HAS LEARNED TO FEAR THE STEEL MASK THAT HIDES THE RAVAGED FEATURES OF VICTOR VON DOOM...

...OR THE LEATHERY COUNTENANCE OF THE TIME-TRAVELER WHO CALLS HIMSELF KANG.

THERE HAS BEEN THE COLD, ROBOTIC FORM OF ULTRON, AND THE BIONIC MONSTROSITY THAT IS DOCTOR OCTOPUS.

BUT FOR THE BAND OF MUTANT TEENAGERS KNOWN AS THE UNCANNY X-MEN, THERE IS ONE SHAPE, ONE FORM, WHICH STRIKES FEAR MORE DEEPLY IN THEIR HEARTS AND SOULS THAN ANY OTHER.

THE SLEEKLY STYLIZED HELMET OF THE SELF-PROCLAIMED EVIL MUTANT, **MAGNETO!**

IT IS PERFECT, MASTER! PERFECT!

IT IS FAR FROM THAT, AMPHIBIUS.

BUT FOR NOW, IT WILL SUFFICE!

JOHN BYRNE AND **TOM PALMER**
WRITER - ARTISTS

GREG WRIGHT
COLORIST

JASON LIEBIG
EDITOR

BOB HARRAS
EDITOR IN CHIEF

THE PLACE IS A HIDDEN GROTTO, ON A SMALL ISLAND OFF THE COAST OF THE SAVAGE LAND.

THE MAN IS THE SAME OF WHOM WE HAVE BUT RECENTLY SPOKEN. MAGNETO HIMSELF.

THE OTHER IS ONE WHO WAS A MAN, BUT WHO HAS BEEN TRANSFORMED BY HIS MASTER'S PERVERSIONS OF SCIENCE INTO SOMETHING ELSE.

TIME AND CIRCUMSTANCE HAVE COMBINED TO ROB ME OF MY TRUE, ALL-CONQUERING COLORS...

...BUT WITH SUCH RAW MATERIALS AS THIS PLACE PROVIDES...

...I HAVE BEEN ABLE TO CRAFT AN ACCEPTABLE REPLACEMENT.

CLOSE ENOUGH, AT LEAST, THAT THOSE WHO ARE ABOUT TO DIE BY MY HAND...

"...WILL KNOW IN THE LAST MOMENTS OF THEIR LIVES WHO IT IS WHO DESTROYS THEM!"

YOU KNOW—MAYBE IT'S MY AMNESIA AFFECTING THE WAY MY WHOLE BRAIN WORKS...

...BUT I JUST REALIZED YOU NEVER HAVE TOLD ME YOUR NAME!

SINCE YOU WERE AND ARE UNABLE TO TELL ME YOURS, THE QUESTION HAS NOT COME UP.

IF YOU WISH, HOWEVER, YOU MAY CALL ME... JOE SMITH.

REALLY? DON'T HAVE TOO MUCH TROUBLE REGISTERING AT HOTELS WITH A NAME LIKE THAT, DO YOU?

NO OFFENSE, BUT IT SOUNDS KINDA FAKE!

WHETHER IT DOES OR NOT IS OF LITTLE CONCERN TO ME.

YOU ASKED FOR A NAME, AND I HAVE GIVEN ONE.

ONE WHICH WILL CHANCE TO STIR NO MEMORY WITHIN YOUR DAMAGED BRAIN.

SOMETHING WHICH MIGHT WELL OCCUR, SHOULD I TELL YOU I AM KARL LYKOS!

...WE MUST TURN OUR EYES FOR A MOMENT TO THIS PLACE ALMOST AS FAR FROM OUR STARTING POINT AS THE SURFACE OF THE EARTH WILL ALLOW.

SUBURBAN DUNFEE, ILLINOIS.

SPECIFICALLY THE BACK YARD OF THIS ONCE PEACEFUL DOMICILE...

...WHERE LATELY NIGHTMARE, IT WOULD SEEM HAS TAKEN UP RESIDENCE...

A-ASHLEY? BABY, ARE YOU OKAY..?

CAREFUL, MRS. MARTIN! THAT *IS* YOUR *DAUGHTER,* TO BE SURE...

...BUT SHE IS PRESENTLY THE CENTER OF FORCES NONE OF US CAN YET BEGIN TO COMPREHEND!

TH-THAT *GIANT ROBOT!* SHE... SHE MADE IT TEAR ITSELF APART!

THAT WAS ITS OWN STUPID FAULT!

I THOUGHT IT WAS MY *FRIEND.* BUT IT *ATTACKED* ME!*

*ALL SEEN IN OUR PREVIOUS ISSUE - J

THIS IS ALL BECAUSE *YOU* CAME HERE, ISN'T IT!

BIG BOT WAS JUST *FINE* UNTIL *YOU* SHOWED UP..!

IT IS *TRUE* OUR PRESENCE TRIGGERED THE SENTINEL'S MUTANT-HUNTING CIRCUITRY, ASHLEY...

...BUT I FEAR IT WAS ONLY A MATTER OF *TIME* BEFORE YOUR OWN *NASCENT* MUTANT POWERS WOULD HAVE DONE THE SAME...

"SOMETHING MUCH MORE DANGEROUS."

AND SPEAKING OF THE DISTAFF MEMBER OF THE ORIGINAL X-MEN TEAM...

WEIGH ANCHOR!

WE'LL WAIT OUT HERE FOR THEM TO COME TO US!

...ON A STRANGE, DARK SHIP, MANY MILES FROM THE FAMILIAR SHORES OF THE X-MEN'S NEW YORK HOME...

TOO BAD KRUEGER HAD TO USE HIS POWER TO KNOCK OUT YOU AND THE OTHER MUTIES, MARVEL GIRL.

PRETTY LITTLE THING LIKE YOU DON'T COME ON BOARD THIS OL' RUST-BUCKET NONE TOO OF'N!

I'M SURE!

YOU'RE CONSCIOUS? THAT'S...

UNGH!

NEXT WORD "IMPOSSIBLE" BY ANY CHANCE?

MAYBE... BUT IN THE SHORT TIME I'VE BEEN HANGING AROUND WITH THE X-MEN...

"...I'VE LEARNED TO BE VERY CAREFUL ABOUT WHAT I CALL 'IMPOSSIBLE!'"

HERE THEY COME.

I CAN SEE THAT FOR MYSELF, BLUNT. BE CAREFUL THAT YOU DO NOT LET YOUR ENTHUSIASM OVERWHELM YOU.

BUT, AS I TOLD MAGNETO, I HAVE FOUND A KIND OF PEACE HERE.

SO, I HAVE SIMPLY REMOVED FROM YOUR MEMORIES ALL KNOWLEDGE OF WHAT TRANSPIRED HERE.

YOU DID NOT MEET MAGNETO HERE, YOU DID NOT BATTLE SAURON.

YOU SIMPLY...

...FOUND YOU THERE! IF CEREBRO HADN'T SIGNALED US...

...I WOULD HAVE HAD A LONG WALK HOME!

AND YOU MIGHT YET, IF YOU DON'T SIT DOWN AND STRAP IN! I'M POWERING THIS BABY UP TO FULL SPEED!

LUCKY THIS FLYER WASN'T TOO BADLY DAMAGED BY THE LANDING.

STILL CAN'T THINK WHAT MADE THE POWER CUT OUT LIKE THAT! AH, WELL...

"...MAYBE THE PROF CAN FIGURE IT OUT WHEN WE GET HOME."

GONE!

ALL GONE!

THE X-MEN.

SAURON.

MAGNETO.

ALL THE DREAMS ARE ENDED, THEN. ALL THE HOPES ARE DASHED.

ALL THAT REMAINS IS TO FIND A WAY HOME--HOME TO THE EMPTINESS THAT WAS MY LIFE AS A SAVAGE IN A SAVAGE LAND...

AND WITH MAGNETO GONE, SO TOO AT LAST IS THE POWER WHICH KEPT ME IN MY MUTATE FORM.

THE END..?

NOT QUITE...

HE BREATHES. THAT IS WHY THE SCAVENGERS HAD NOT YET PICKED CLEAN HIS BONES!

I MUST TAKE HIM TO ATLANTIS, WHILE THE FLAME OF LIFE STILL FLICKERS.

YET I FEEL UPON ME A GREAT SENSE OF FOREBODING.

THIS MORTAL IS KNOWN TO ME, AND SUCH DEALINGS AS WE HAVE HAD IN THE PAST...

...HAVE LEFT ME WITH LITTLE URGE TO TRUST HIM.

SO DOES THE SUB-MARINER LEAVE BEHIND THE BATTLEFIELD...

...NEVER GUESSING THE DEADLY GAME WHICH HAS BEEN PLAYED HERE.

LEAST OF ALL THE MUTANT CALLED MAGNETO!

SO MUST I BE CAUTIOUS, LEST HIS SLY AND SERPENTINE MACHINATIONS LEAD ME DOWN A PATH TO RUINATION.

NAMOR OF ATLANTIS IS NEVER TO BE THE DUPE OF ANY MAN...

NO MORE THAN HE CAN GUESS WHAT LIES BUT A FEW SHORT HOURS AHEAD...*

*WHAT LIES AHEAD FOR NAMOR IS LONG AGO FOR US -- THE CATACLYSMIC CONTENTS OF FANTASTIC FOUR #102!

FOR US, HOWEVER, WHAT LIES AHEAD IS OUR OWN NEXT ISSUE, AND A CHILLING TALE OF VENGEANCE WE COULD ONLY CALL...

BLOOD and CIRCUSES

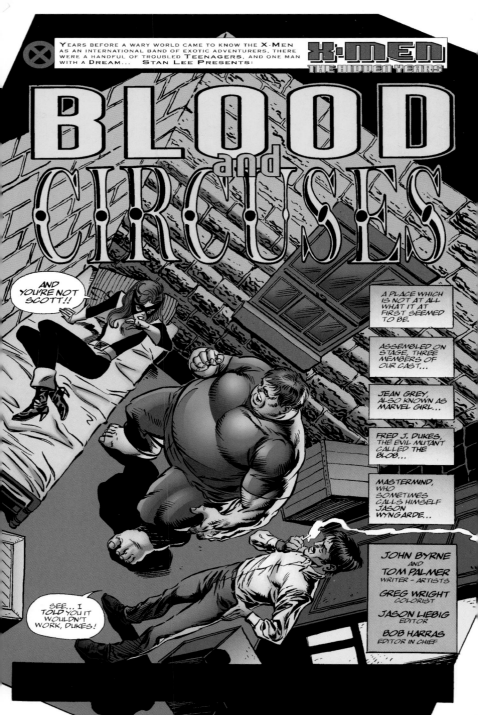

STILL, IT'S A SAFE BET YOU'RE ABOUT AS BOGUS AS A SYMPATHY CARD FROM MAGNETO!

...OTHER X-MEN HAVE TROUBLES OF THEIR OWN.

HER POWER IS *INCREDIBLE* FOR A CHILD OF TEN!

SHE'S MANIPULATING THE SHATTERED *HULK* OF THAT SENTINEL AS THOUGH IT WERE NOTHING BUT A *MARIONETTE!*

WHERE'S *JEANIE* IN ALL THIS?

...WAS THAT REALLY HER WITH THE BLOB AND UNUS...?

AS THESE THOUGHTS TROUBLE THE MAN CALLED CYCLOPS...

NOT SURPRISING, SINCE IT WAS THIS VERY POWER WHICH COMPELLED THE MECHANICAL MENACE TO LITERALLY *TEAR ITSELF APART!* ※

PROFESSOR! THERE'S *NOTHING* I CAN DO TO *CONTAIN* THIS THING!

IS THERE *ANYTHING* YOU CAN *DO?*

※IN X-HY #11 – J

THERE IS...

BUT I DREAD THE CONSEQUENCES!

OH, YOU *DO,* DO YOU?

"...AND THE LAST THING WE WANT TO DO IS KILL ANYBODY!!!

WELL, WITHOUT MASTERMIND'S ILLUSIONS AT WORK, THIS FALLS A LONG WAY SHORT OF THE SWANKEST LODGINGS I'VE EVER HAD!

BUT IT DOESN'T MAKE FOR MUCH OF A JAIL CELL, EITHER!

EVERYTHING IS SO OLD AND DIRTY I THINK I CAN SAFELY ASSUME NONE OF THIS IS MASTERMIND'S DOING!

BUT THAT DOESN'T HELP ME FIND...

THIS WOULD BE A LOT EASIER IF THERE WAS A CONVENIENT KEY I COULD FLOAT INTO THE LOCK WITH MY TELEKINESIS...

...BUT SINCE THERE ISN'T, I'LL JUST HAVE TO DO WHAT I CAN WITH THE INNER WORKINGS OF THE LOCK.

...FIND...

OH-HH...!

THERE!

LUCKY IT WAS A SIMPLE MECHANISM! A LOCKPICK I AIN'T!

CENTERPORT, LONG ISLAND.

THE WORTHINGTON ESTATE, LISTED WHERE SUCH THINGS MATTER AS ONE OF THE FIVE GREATEST HOUSES IN THE NATION.

THANK YOU, DARLING.

I CAN'T TELL YOU OFTEN ENOUGH WHAT A COMFORT YOU'VE BEEN TO ME.

IS IT ANY WONDER I FELL IN LOVE WITH YOU?

..A MIRROR OF MY OWN FEELINGS FOR YOU, KATHRYN.

YOU KNOW I HAVE BEEN IN LOVE WITH YOU SINCE THE FIRST MOMENT WARREN INTRODUCED US.

I COULD NOT BELIEVE HIS GOOD FORTUNE, THAT HE SHOULD HAVE FOUND YOU FIRST.

LET'S.. NOT SPEAK OF THAT BURTRAM.

WHEN I THINK OF MY HUSBAND, IT ALL BECOMES SO PAINFUL. I START TO THINK.. HOW WE'RE RUSHING THINGS..

YOU MUSTN'T THINK THAT, DEAREST. MY DEAR BROTHER WOULD NOT WANT YOU TO MOURN FOREVER.

YOU ARE STILL A YOUNG WOMAN--YOU HAVE A LIFETIME BEFORE YOU.

WITH ME.

YES.. WITH YOU, DEAR, DEAR, BURTRAM.

I ONLY WISH MY SON COULD BE HERE FOR THE WEDDING..

NEXT

MOTHER and CHILD REUNION

HE'S **RIGHT!** LOOK AT THIS PLACE!

I THOUGHT WE WUZ WORKIN' FOR SOMEBODY BIGGER'N BARNUM AND BAILEY...

..BUT THIS PLACE AIN'T NOTHIN' BUT SAWDUST AND OLD CANVAS!

WANNA BET THE **MONEY** WE BIN PAID AIN'T NO BETTER?

WHATEVER! IT WASN'T ENOUGH TO TAKE NO **REAL** BRUISIN' FROM THESE FREAKS!

RUN! LET 'EM FIGHT THEIR OWN FIGHTS!!

THAT WAS ALMOST TOO EASY!

NOW WHERE ARE OUR HOSTS? IF THEIR POWERS ARE SHUT OFF, TOO...

WARREN-- LOOK! OVER THERE...!

IT **IS** KRUEGER! AND HE'S GOT JEAN!

DON'T COME ANY CLOSER, X-MEN.

REMEMBER, MY POWER CAN **KILL** AS EASILY AS IT CAN **DISABLE!**

"...I'LL SECOND THAT EMOTION."

THE POOR KID IS JUST *BEAT!*

NOT SURPRISING, I GUESS, GIVEN WHAT SHE'S BEEN THROUGH SINCE LEAVING THE SAVAGE LAND!

GUESS WE SHOULD TAKE HER *BACK* THERE, HUH?

ALL IN FAVOR OF A SIDE TRIP TO ANTARCTICA...

NOT JUST YET, WARREN.

IN CASE YOU'VE FORGOTTEN, I'M NOT JUST TAGGING ALONG HERE BECAUSE I THINK I LOOK GOOD IN GREEN.

I CAME LOOKING FOR *YOU*-BECAUSE I HAVE SOMETHING *IMPORTANT* TO TELL YOU.

IF YOU TWO NEED SOME *PRIVACY*...

NO, CYCLOPS, YOU AND MARVEL GIRL SHOULD PROBABLY HEAR THIS, TOO.

SEE--IT INVOLVES WHAT I GUESS YOU'D CALL A *SUPER VILLAIN.* ONE THAT WARREN AND I HAD A *RUN-IN* WITH A WHILE BACK.

ONE WHO'S ABOUT TO MARRY ANGEL'S *MOTHER!*

THAT'S YOUR LOT, FOLKS. BUT YOU WON'T HAVE TO WAIT LONG FOR MORE X-ACTION, 'COS THE FINAL X-MEN: THE HIDDEN YEARS POCKETBOOK *WORLDS WITHIN WORLDS* WILL BE COMING SOON!